★ THE MOVIES

by Joanne Mattern

HOUGHTON MIFFLIN HARCOURT
School Publishers

PHOTOGRAPHY CREDITS: Cover © image100/Alamy; tp © Bettmann/Corbis; 3 © image100/Alamy; 5 © Bettmann/Corbis; 6 (t) © Bettmann/Corbis; 6 (b) © Corbis; 8 © Paris Claude/Corbis SYGMA; 9, 10 © Bettmann/Corbis; 12 © Swim Ink 2, LLC/Corbis; 13 © TWPhoto/Corbis.

Printed in China

ISBN-13: 978-0-547-01875-1
ISBN-10: 0-547-01875-4

9 10 11 0940 18 17 16 15 14 13
4500416928

TABLE OF CONTENTS

Step inside the museum of movie magic! You'll find all sorts of wonders here.

Everyone enjoys a good movie. For more than one hundred years, movies have told stories that people love. Some movies are funny, and some are sad. Others are filled with **thrilling** special effects that leave you on the edge of your seat.

Let's take a walk through our museum and learn how technology has changed the way movies tell stories.

Millions of people watch movies every year.

THE VERY FIRST MOVIE

The first movie was made way back in 1888. In October of that year, a man named Louis Le Prince made a movie called *Roundhay Garden Scene.*

At the time, Le Prince's movie was very new and very different. No one had seen anything like it. The focus of the short film is four actors who walk around a garden, talking and laughing with each other. Most films made today last at least ninety minutes, but this one lasts only two seconds!

Le Prince filmed his movie using a camera he had invented. It filmed only ten to twelve frames per second. Images from the camera lens were transferred to a two-inch roll of paper. This roll of paper was turned into a negative.

Thomas Edison helped to develop the early movie industry.

The parts of pictures that seem dark on a negative will show up bright when light is placed behind the negative. The bright parts of a negative show up as dark. So, what you see in a movie is actually the opposite of what is on the negative!

During the early 1890s, a new material called celluloid began to be used widely to make films. Celluloid is a type of plastic. When it is coated with a special gelatin, celluloid can hold images projected onto it by a camera.

Celluloid was cut into strips. The strips were then threaded into a projector to show the movie. However, it was hard to keep the celluloid strips from sliding around and making the film jolt and jump. Inventors soon found a better way by cutting holes in the sides of each strip. The projector then held the newly perforated film in place.

EARLY INVENTIONS

Here's the next exhibit. You have heard of Thomas Edison because he invented the light bulb and the record player. But guess what? He also invented a lot of new technology for the movies!

Kinetoscope

Kinetograph

In 1893, Edison showed two amazing new inventions to the public. The first invention was the kinetograph. The second was the kinetoscope.

The kinetograph was the first practical motion picture camera. Celluloid film was threaded onto turning disks inside the kinetograph. As the wheels turned, the film moved.

The kinetoscope was a large cabinet. People looked into it through a hole and watched the movie playing inside. The movie itself was a fifty-foot-long loop of film that played over and over. A magnifying glass and a lamp inside the kinetoscope helped people see each frame.

Soon, kinetoscope parlors opened up around the country. Each person paid twenty-five cents to look into a kinetoscope. There was still no way to show the movie to a large group, but that would soon change.

In 1895, Auguste Lumière and his brother Louis invented a movie projector called the cinematograph. This was a camera, printer, and projector all in one. The Lumiéres began showing simple movies in Paris.

People in other countries were also beginning to show movies to the public. These films were short, and there was no fancy editing or camera movement. However, people rushed to see these "moving pictures."

The Lumières' films were projected onto a screen.

George Méliès' short film, *A Trip to the Moon*, was the first movie about space travel.

As time passed, movies became more creative. In 1902, George Méliès made a movie called *A Trip to the Moon*. The movie was only eight minutes long, but it told a story about a group of adventurers who manage to travel to the moon. Méliès used many new tricks that made his movie ==entertaining==. He was also one of the first to ==advertise== his movie so people would want to see it. The movie became famous and can still be seen today.

During the 1920s, a sound system for movies called the Vitaphone sound-on-disc system was created. The Vitaphone had a projector and a record player that worked together. In 1927, a performer named Al Jolson appeared in the most famous of the Vitaphone movies, *The Jazz Singer*. Eventually, a better system was developed that had the sound recorded on the same film as the pictures. Talking pictures had arrived!

Thousands came to see *The Jazz Singer*.

Directors began to use different camera angles to tell a story. They also began to film several different scenes and then edit them together. This created excitement and drama.

Early movies were shown only in black and white, but by the 1950s, color film was available. Also by this time, Hollywood, California had become the movie-making capital of the world.

In 1953, a Hollywood movie studio called Twentieth Century Fox introduced CinemaScope. This was a way to show movies on a wide screen. In the past, the images on film were distorted if they were stretched onto a wide screen. CinemaScope solved this problem by using two lenses. The first lens captured the image. The second lens fixed the distortion. Cinemascope also featured stereo sound. Now the sound was as big as the picture!

By this time, movies were a huge industry. Movie studios spent a lot of money to make movies. Studios also spent millions to promote and advertise them. In addition, critics began to review movies. A good review could make the difference between success and failure for the movie.

SPECIAL EFFECTS!

Special effects became popular in the 1930s. A machine called an optical printer allowed two movies to be put onto one piece of film, becoming one movie. The optical printer made it possible to create movies like the 1933 version of *King Kong*.

The special effects in *King Kong* were so spectacular that the film is still popular today.

There are many jobs available in the movie business for people who are good with computers.

In the 1970s and 1980s, movies like *Star Wars* and the *Indiana Jones* series generated excitement through fantastic space battles and thrilling scenes of danger.

Movie technology changed during the 1990s. For the first time, studios used digital technology to create special effects. In time, entire movies were created using computers.

Children are the target audience for many movies created by computers. The first feature-length movie that was animated entirely by computer was called *Toy Story*. This movie is told from the point of view of the toys in one boy's bedroom.

The next generation of cinema magicians is growing up right now. Children and teens are comfortable with digital technology and are always eager to see something new. Who knows what breakthroughs you might make in the years to come!

KEY EVENTS IN THE MAKING OF MOVIES

1888 • The first officially recognized movie, *Roundhay Garden Scene*, is made.

1893 • Thomas Edison shows his kinetograph and kinetoscope to the public.

1895 • Auguste and Louis Lumière invent the cinematograph and begin showing movies in Paris.

1902 • George Méliès makes a movie called *A Trip to the Moon*.

1927 • *The Jazz Singer* is released.

1933 • *King Kong* introduces moviegoers to special effects.

1953 • CinemaScope creates a wide screen effect.

1970s • *Star Wars* introduces improved special effects.

1995 • *Toy Story*, the first movie animated entirely by computer, is released.

Responding

 TARGET SKILL **Fact and Opinion** Can you find places where the author presented facts in this story? Can you find places where she has presented opinions? Copy and complete the chart below.

Facts	Opinions
The first movie was made back in 1888. ?	Everyone enjoys a good movie. ?

 **Write About It**

Text to World Write a one-paragraph review of a movie you have seen recently. Be sure to include facts about the movie as well as your opinions about what you felt was good and bad about the movie.

advertise	generated
angles	jolts
critics	promote
entertaining	target
focus	thrilling

TARGET SKILL **Fact and Opinion** Decide if an idea can be proved or if it is a feeling or belief.

TARGET STRATEGY **Summarize** Briefly tell the important parts of the text in your own words.

GENRE **Informational Text** gives facts and examples about a topic.